D0518623

Touching

Paul Humphrey

Photography by Chris Fairclough

W
FRANKLIN WATTS
LONDON•SYDNEY

First published in 2007 by
Franklin Watts
338 Euston Road
London NW1 3BH

Franklin Watts Australia
Level 17/207 Kent Street
Sydney NSW 2000

© 2007 Franklin Watts

ISBN: 978 0 7496 7451 9 (hbk)
ISBN: 978 0 7496 7463 2 (pbk)

Dewey classification number: 612.8'8

A CIP catalogue record for this book is available
from the British Library.

Planning and production by Discovery Books Limited
Editor: Rachel Tisdale
Designer: Ian Winton
Photography: Chris Fairclough
Series advisors: Diana Bentley MA and Dee Reid MA,
Fellows of Oxford Brookes University

The author, packager and publisher would like to thank the following
people for their participation in this book: Auriel and Ottilie Austin-Baker, Bryn
Stallard-Pearson, Harriet and Imogen Stanley, Lucas Tisdale, the students and
teachers of Penn Hall School, Wolverhampton.

Printed in China

Franklin Watts is a division of Hachette Children's Books.

Contents

Five senses

You have five senses.
They are seeing,
touching, hearing,
smelling and tasting.

Touching

Seeing

Hearing

Smelling

Tasting

5

Touching

You often use your hands to touch things.

But you can touch
things with any part
of your body.

Rough and smooth

When you touch things, you can feel if they are rough...

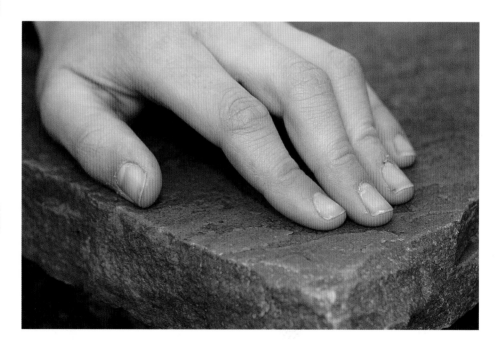

...or smooth.

9

Hot and cold

You can tell if things
are hot...

...or cold.

Soft and prickly

Some things
feel soft.

Some things feel prickly.

Some things feel sticky.

Head and feet

You can feel a soft pillow under your head.

You can feel
scrunchy sand
under your feet.

Wet and dry

You can feel if things are wet...

...or dry.

17

Nice and nasty

Some things are nice to touch.

Some things are
nasty to touch.

Using touch

Blind people touch things to find out what they are like.

They can even feel words to read.

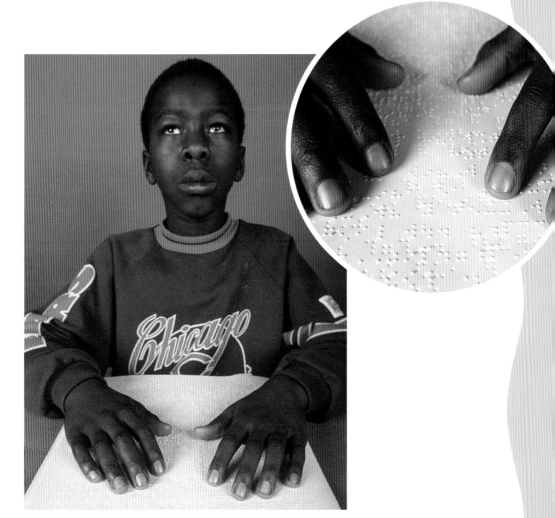

Hello and goodbye

We touch to say hello.

We touch to
say goodbye.

Word bank

Look back for these words and pictures.

Blind people

Body

Cold

Dry

Hands

Hot

Prickly

Rough

Scrunchy

Smooth

Sticky

Wet